ETERNAL FAMILY STRUCTURES AMONG EXALTED COUPLES

ILYAN KEI LAVANWAY

Ilyan Kei Lavanway
Lehigh, Kansas

Dedicated to my sister, Tia Rex

Thank you, Tia, for your input regarding Doctrine and Covenants 132:50-52. Your observations were instrumental in helping me solidify my thoughts on the subject of how eternal family structures might be organized among exalted couples. I love you.

This page intentionally left blank.

CONTENTS

This page intentionally left blank.

AUTHOR'S NOTE

My reference to Tinker Toys is not in any way intended to speak irreverently of the sacred nature of eternal families and the ordinances of the Holy Priesthood and the atonement of Jesus Christ that make eternal families possible. Years ago, while pondering, I had an epiphany. Imagining exalted couples forming eternal families, Tinker Toys popped into my head. My simple mind could not think of what else to call it.

It was not until three years after I had conceptualized the basic pattern shown in **Illustration-1** included in this written work that I visited the Oklahoma City Temple for the first time in my life. As I was waiting in the sealing room to serve as proxy to seal one of my ancestors to his parents, I noticed the pattern in the carpet of the sealing room floor.

That pattern of circles joined by lines forming squares is strikingly similar to the patterns I had imagined three years prior, while thinking about how eternal families might be structured among exalted couples. The concept of this structure solidified in my mind with great clarity while studying the first chapter of Matthew. Surely, I cannot be the only one to discover this.

This page intentionally left blank.

PREFACE

Let me preface these thoughts by acknowledging that we have been asked to share some of our personal insights during Sunday school discussions. The thoughts expressed in this written work are my own. I believe they are personal revelations from the Holy Ghost to me, as an individual.

These thoughts are not intended as revelations for any Sunday school class, Seminary class, or Institute class, or for any Stake or Ward or Branch, or for the Church. These thoughts are not intended to be authoritative, definitive, or final. They are a personal work in progress.

I am learning by study and also by faith. I may err, and I am subject to correction. That correction, when it is needed, may come through other individuals, but must be confirmed to me by the Holy Ghost.

Varying opinions will arise. However, based on my current understanding of the scriptures, and the whisperings of the Holy Ghost to my own soul, I am convinced the following thoughts have merit.

This page intentionally left blank.

PERSONAL INSIGHTS ON THE FIRST CHAPTER OF MATTHEW

I find it interesting that the genealogy of Jesus Christ, recorded in the first chapter of Matthew, is actually the genealogy of Joseph, mortal husband of Mary. Biologically, Christ's mortal and spiritual *paternal* lineage is Heavenly Father.

This fact implies Mary has two husbands: Heavenly Father and Joseph. It has to be. Heavenly Father delights in the chastity of women (see Jacob 2:28), and would not have sired a child out of wedlock. Joseph was a righteous man and would not have taken Mary outside the covenant of eternal marriage. The fact that Mary and Joseph had children together after the birth of Christ makes it clear that Joseph and Mary were husband and wife. Their children must have been born in the covenant of eternal marriage.

Jesus is the biological and spiritual son of Heavenly Father, and the biological son of Mary. Mary has to be a wife of Heavenly Father, married to Heavenly Father in the covenant of eternal marriage, because Jesus cannot be a bastard child.

How could Jesus set the perfect example if his mortal life were to have begun as an illegitimate child?

My sister, Tia, discovered a detail related to this in Doctrine and Covenants 132:50-52:

"*50 Behold, I have seen your sacrifices, and will forgive all your sins; I have seen your sacrifices in obedience to that which I have told you. Go, therefore, and I make a way for your escape, as I accepted the offering of Abraham of his son Isaac.*

"*51 Verily, I say unto you: A commandment I give unto mine handmaid, Emma Smith, your wife, whom I have given unto you, that she stay herself and partake not of that which I commanded you to offer unto her; for I did it, saith the Lord, to prove you all, as I did Abraham, and that I might require an offering at your hand, by covenant and sacrifice.*

"*52 And let mine handmaid, Emma Smith, receive all those that have been given unto my servant Joseph, and who are virtuous and pure before me; and those who are not pure, and have said they were pure, shall be destroyed, saith the Lord God.*"

I believe the sacrifice Joseph Smith was to offer to Emma was to give her multiple husbands. This, for Joseph Smith, would have been as great a trial of faith as Abraham being asked to sacrifice his son, Isaac. Once the willingness to make these sacrifices was manifest, the Lord made an escape from the requirement to go through with them. The necessary faith had been demonstrated in the willingness and intent to humbly obey without murmuring or reviling.

Would men in the Church today obey if commanded by the Lord to give our wives additional husbands while we are still alive and married? Perhaps we should humble ourselves and be willing, if such were ever to be the case.

Many of us men secretly, or not so secretly, expect our wives to be willing to accept the possibility that at some point in our eternal exaltation, we are going to have multiple wives.

I wonder if any men in the Church of Jesus Christ of Latter-day Saints today have ever pondered the precedent set by Mary having two husbands, and confirmed by the apparent scriptural account of Joseph Smith being asked to give his wife, Emma, multiple husbands while he and Emma were both still alive.

When I shared these thoughts with my Dad, Victor Gordon LaVanway, he made at least three inspired observations:

One: such a commandment, or even the very knowledge of this subject matter, would prove the hearts of men, and might have a cleansing effect on the Church as a whole. In other words, it would weed out from among the truly faithful those not willing to sacrifice their pride, emotions, intellectual prowess, or mortal paradigm.

Two: this system has an infinite practicality in bringing to pass the immortality and eternal life of the countless human intelligences awaiting spirit bodies.

Three: he would not want to disturb anyone's Gospel equilibrium before they are ready to receive a truth.

ETERNAL FAMILY STRUCTURES AMONG EXALTED COUPLES

I believe these are types and shadows of eternal family structures among exalted persons. I visualize this idea using what I call the Tinker Toy Model of Eternal Family Structures.

Picture the little round, wooden wheels — let's call them nodes — with the little holes in them. Let's paint some nodes pink and some nodes blue. The pink nodes are exalted wives. The blue nodes are exalted husbands.

Now, make an exalted couple by connecting one pink node to one blue node with a stick fitted into a hole on each node. Let the stick represent the covenant bond of eternal marriage. Clip some clothes pins onto the stick that joins the pink node to the blue node. The clothes pins represent spirit children born to the husband and wife who are connected by the covenant of eternal marriage.

Now, connect another pink node to the blue node with a second stick at a ninety degree angle to the first stick. Clip some clothes pins on that stick. Now we have a husband with two wives, and spirit children with distinct lineages. There is no mistaking which spirit child comes from which parents.

Attach another blue node to one of the pink nodes with a third stick, making an open-sided square. Now, we have a wife with two husbands. Clip some clothes pins onto that third stick. The spirit children begotten by each exalted couple are clearly connected to one and only one set of heavenly parents. There is no confusion. There is order. There is a specific, identifiable lineage and heritage for each spirit child.

Link the blue and pink nodes at the open side of the square with a fourth stick, completing one square. The square should have two blue nodes situated diagonally from one another and not sharing a stick. The two pink nodes should be situated diagonally from one another and not sharing a stick. There is only a stick between a blue node and a pink node. There is never a stick joining two blue nodes to each other. There is never a stick joining two pink nodes to each other.

Now, repeat this process in a plane perpendicular to the first square, until you have completed one cube. Notice that each husband has three wives, and each wife has three husbands, but there is no confusion. There is order. Each and every spirit child has a specific, identifiable lineage. Each spirit child has exactly one set of exalted parents.

Keep adding cubes to each side of the first cube, and then more cubes to each side of those additional cubes, expanding outward to infinity. This represents eternal increase, and a structurally strong and stable family. The more this pattern is added upon, the stronger it gets, and never is there any confusion. There is order. Every spirit child is begotten by a distinctly identifiable, single set of heavenly parents.

Never are two husbands linked to each other. Never are two wives linked to each other. The pattern is the same no matter how big the structure grows. Males are only connected to females. Females are only connected to males. Every spirit child has exactly one set of exalted parents.

See **Illustration-1** for a visual representation of this exercise.

If we expand this pattern of cubes indefinitely, we can see that each husband has exactly six wives, and each wife has exactly six husbands. There is a balance.

Let's not stop here. We are talking about eternal increase, and we already know there is a hastening, an acceleration, involved in Heavenly Father's work and glory, which is to bring to pass the immortality and eternal life of man.

Add one cube within each cube, making a network of hypercubes. To help visualize this, picture each cube in **Illustration-1** as being a hypercube like the one shown close up in **Illustration-2**.

Pick any node at any corner of one of the cubes in **Illustration-1**. Count how many nodes of opposite gender are directly attached to it. There are six nodes of opposite gender attached to it from the regular cubes, counting up-down, left-right, front-back. Now it gets interesting.

There are eight more nodes of opposite gender attached to the same node, when counting the eight inner portions of the hypercubes.

Remember, when counting the inner portions of adjacent hypercubes, there will be a back-upper-left, back-upper-right, back-lower-left, back-lower-right, front-upper-left, front-upper-right, front-lower-left, front-lower-right.

Notice that each husband has exactly fourteen wives, and each wife has exactly fourteen husbands. Does Matthew 1:17 hint of this?

See **Illustration-2** for a visual representation of this exercise.

We can continue adding hypercubes within hypercubes within hypercubes, ad infinitum.

Take it even further. Look at each square in its own plane. There is a node at each corner. Add one node of opposite gender to each node of the square, forming a coplanar rectangle inside the square.

For each square, we can add any number of coplanar rectangles in similar manner. Never are nodes of the same gender connected to each other.

Examining even one square at a time, we can see that each husband may have infinitely many wives, and each wife may have infinitely many husbands, as long as a pattern is followed.

If the pattern is followed, there is never confusion. There is order. Every spirit child has exactly one set of heavenly parents. Males are never married to males. Females are never married to females.

See **Illustration-3** for a visual representation of this exercise.

I believe the principle of eternal increase not only refers to infinitely many spirit offspring, but also to infinitely many eternal spouses. Simple geometry seems to prove this profound possibility.

Now, consider that each blue node — each exalted husband — is the patriarch of his own godhead. His firstborn spirit child will be the atoning agent for all of his spirit offspring throughout all eternity, regardless of which of his wives bears them.

Each atoning agent must be the firstling of his *father*. An atoning agent is not referred to as the firstling of his mother. This lends itself to a simple patriarchal order. The first spirit child born to a given heavenly mother is not necessarily the first spirit child born to that mother's husband.

Each patriarch will preside over the creation of infinitely many earths throughout all eternity. The firstling of each patriarch will be the creator of the heavens and earths his father directs him to create. To each distinct earth, a specific group of spirit offspring will be assigned for mortal probation (see *Nature of the Godhead* by Ilyan Kei Lavanway, ISBN 9780463012000).

I believe one perfect male spirit offspring will be assigned as a testifying agent and ordained to the office of holy ghost for the inhabitants of each separate and distinct earth.

The inhabitants of all the earths created by a given atoning agent — firstling — will have the same heavenly father, whom they will worship in the name of his firstling.

However, each distinct earth will have a separate holy ghost assigned as testifying agent specifically to that earth's inhabitants.

See **Illustration-4** for a visual representation of this concept.

One earth out of all the earths created by a given firstling will be the footstool earth, the earth upon which the firstling carries out his mortal ministry and completes his atonement, applicable to all his father's spirit offspring, forever more.

The atonement of any given firstling will have infinite scope and eternal efficacy, strictly and exclusively applicable to the spirit offspring of that firstling's father, and *not* applicable to the spirit offspring of any other father.

Each father will have infinitely many and ever increasing spirit posterity, so each father's firstling's atonement must have infinite reach, and must remain effective throughout all eternity.

While pondering the special relationship between firstlings and their respective fathers, I gained a deeper appreciation for what it means for the Father and the Firstling to be one.

"And that I am in the Father, and the Father in me, and the Father and I are one" (Doctrine and Covenants 93:3)

Each firstling only atones for his own father's spirit offspring.

Even though many of that father's spirit offspring come from mothers who have husbands in addition to the firstling's father, only those spirit children who have the same father as the firstling come under that firstling's atonement.

By definition, there is only one firstling per father, and so there is only one atoning agent for all the spirit children of a given father.

An exalted mother may have spirit children from many different fathers, so some of her spirit children will have a different atoning agent than others of her spirit children. This fact strikes me with awe and reverence for eternal motherhood.

Interestingly, in spite of the fact that each exalted wife may have multiple exalted husbands, the entire family structure among exalted couples forms an infinitely vast and ever expanding network that functions as a patriarchal order.

Indeed, the entire structure cannot function in any manner other than a patriarchal order. Each firstling is the firstling of one and only one father.

As far as the role of atoning agent is concerned, a firstling is never referred to as the firstling of a mother. Each and every atoning agent is known as the firstling of his father.

In our thought exercise using Tinker Toys as visualization tools, each node representing an exalted father might, in one way, also represent that father's firstling, the atoning agent for all the spirit children begotten by that father.

Perhaps someone might observe the multitudes of spirit children born of a given exalted mother and ask: Who is the atoning agent for all these? The answer is simply: Who is the firstling of the father who begat them?

In other words, look to the father to find the firstling, and look to the firstling to find the father.

Now, one may ask, which wife bears the first spirit child of a given husband?

I don't know. I imagine, in most cases it would be the first wife of that husband, the first wife to whom he was sealed during his mortal probation, or during his time in the spirit world if receiving the matrimonial sealing ordinance for the first time vicariously through proxy temple work.

In other words, the first wife with whom a husband is resurrected and exalted is probably the wife who will clothe the intelligence of that husband's firstling with a spirit body.

"Even those things which were from the beginning before the world was, which were ordained of the Father, through his Only Begotten Son, who was in the bosom of the Father, even from the beginning;" (Doctrine and Covenants 76:13)

I wonder if one of the purposes of the new name is related to the structure and order and organization of eternal families among exalted couples. Perhaps nothing more can be said of this outside the temples.

This page intentionally left blank.

LITERAL REALITY OF DIVINE VIRGIN BIRTH

I also had an impression about the fact that Mary conceived Jesus by the power of the Holy Ghost, and was thus able to become pregnant while remaining a virgin. There is scriptural precedent for what I believe to be a seldom recognized role of the Holy Ghost. I believe one of his roles is to convey matter, including people, from one place to another.

The Holy Ghost baptized Adam, literally carrying him down into the water and then bringing him back out again (see Moses 6:64).

The Holy Ghost physically transported Nephi, son of Helaman, out of the midst of a mob that tried to imprison him (see Helaman 10:16).

The Holy Ghost literally transported the apostle Philip out of the presence of the Ethiopian eunuch he had just baptized (see Acts 8:39-40).

Nephi, son of Lehi, mentions having his body carried by the Holy Ghost to exceedingly high mountains on multiple occasions (see 2 Nephi 4:25; 1 Nephi 11:1).

Mary was transported by the Holy Ghost into the presence of Heavenly Father to conceive Jesus (see 1 Nephi 11:18-20).

If the Holy Ghost can convey an entire person from one place to another, then it is a simple matter for him to convey a sperm cell from Heavenly Father directly into an egg cell in Mary's womb without compromising her virginity.

Perhaps a better explanation of how Mary was able to conceive Jesus without losing her virginity is to consider the fact that a resurrected person can move through mortal matter without disturbing its structural integrity.

For example, after his resurrection, when his disciples were gathered in a room and the doors were shut, Jesus Christ entered the closed room without disturbing the structure of the walls or doors or floor or ceiling (see John 20:19; Luke 24:36-39).

It seems a simple matter, then, for Heavenly Father, being a resurrected, exalted man, to consummate his marriage to Mary while preserving intact her virginity.

The Holy Ghost had to overshadow Mary to keep her from being physically vaporized by the glory of Heavenly Father's presence (see Alma 7:10).

PERSONAL INSIGHTS ON THE FIRST CHAPTER OF LUKE

One of the strongest impressions I had while reading the first chapter of Luke, was how even from his conception in Elizabeth's womb, John the Baptist was fulfilling his mortal ministry to prepare the way before the Savior. Elizabeth was old and had been barren all her life. The people knew it.

Mary was a virgin, and probably in her early teens when the angel Gabriel — the same angel that visited Zacharias six months earlier — appeared to her and explained that she would conceive in her womb the Son of God. Mary was likely as astonished at Gabriel's message to her as Zacharias was at Gabriel's message to him.

I am impressed by Mary — having a child's faith — how she innocently asked the simple question: *How shall this be, seeing I know not a man.* Her question had no disbelief attached to it. Yet the aged Zacharias, who, though blameless before God, and well seasoned in the service of God, had not faith, but doubted when something seemingly impossible was presented to him, even though it was presented to him in the temple by an angel. So great must have been Zacharias' unbelief that the angel removed from Zacharias the ability to speak, and caused that he should remain mute until John the Baptist was born.

John the Baptist was paving the way before Jesus, even from the womb, in that Elizabeth conceiving a child in her old age demonstrated to Mary — and to the people — the simple fact that with God, nothing is impossible. If geriatric Elizabeth who had been barren all her life could become pregnant, then why not a virgin become pregnant? And why not a maiden of lowly station bear the Son of God?

The entire account shows us that by small and simple means, and often through lowliest and weakest of saints, the Lord accomplishes his greatest works in bringing to pass the immorality and eternal life of man.

PERSONAL INSIGHTS ON THE
FIRST CHAPTER OF JOHN

I was excited to learn of Joseph Smith's translation of the first chapter of John:

JST, John 1:1–34 (Compare John 1:1–34)

"The gospel of Jesus Christ has been preached from the beginning. John the Baptist is the Elias who prepares the way for Christ, and Jesus Christ is the Elias who restores all things and through whom salvation comes.

"1 In the beginning was the *gospel preached through the Son. And the gospel was the word,* and the *word* was with the Son, and *the Son was with God,* and the *Son* was *of* God.

"2 The same was in the beginning with God.

"3 All things were made by him; and without him was not anything made which was made.

"4 In him was *the gospel,* and *the gospel was the life,* and the life was the light of men;

"5 And the light shineth *in the world,* and the *world perceiveth* it not.

"6 There was a man sent from God, whose name was John.

"7 The same came *into the world* for a witness, to bear witness of the *light, to bear record of the gospel through the Son, unto all,* that through him *men* might believe.

"8 He was not that *light,* but *came* to bear witness of that *light,*

"9 Which was the *true* light, which lighteth every man *who* cometh into the world;

"10 *Even the Son of God.* He *who* was in the world, and the world was made by him, and the world knew him not.

"11 He came unto his own, and his own received him not.

"12 But as many as received him, to them gave he power to become the sons of God; *only* to them who believe on his name.

"13 *He was* born, not of blood, nor of the will of the flesh, nor of the will of man, but of God.

"14 And the *same word* was made flesh, and dwelt among us, and we beheld his glory, the glory as of the Only Begotten of the Father, full of grace and truth.

"15 John *bear* witness of him, and cried, saying, This *is* he of whom I spake; He who cometh after me, is preferred before me; for he was before me.

"16 *For in the beginning was the Word, even the Son, who is made flesh, and sent unto us by the will of the Father. And as many as believe on his name shall receive of his fullness.* And of his fullness have all we received, *even immortality and eternal life, through his* grace.

"17 For the law was given *through* Moses, but *life* and truth came *through* Jesus Christ.

"18 *For the law was after a carnal commandment, to the administration of death; but the gospel was after the power of an endless life, through Jesus Christ, the Only Begotten Son, who is in the bosom of the Father.*

"19 *And* no man hath seen God at any time, *except he hath borne record of the Son; for except it is through him no man can be saved.*

"20 And this is the record of John, when the Jews sent priests and Levites from Jerusalem, to ask him; Who art thou?

"21 And he confessed, and denied not *that he was Elias;* but confessed, *saying;* I am not the Christ.

"22 And they asked him, *saying; How then art thou Elias?* And he said, I am not *that Elias who was to restore all things.*

And they asked him, saying, Art thou that prophet? And he answered, No.

"23 Then said they unto him, Who art thou? that we may give an answer to them that sent us. What sayest thou of thyself?

"24 He said, I am the voice of one crying in the wilderness, Make straight the way of the Lord, as saith the prophet Esaias.

"25 And they who were sent were of the Pharisees.

"26 And they asked him, and said unto him; Why baptizest thou then, if thou be not the Christ, nor Elias *who was to restore all things,* neither that prophet?

"27 John answered them, saying; I baptize with water, but there standeth one among you, whom ye know not;

"28 He it is *of whom I bear record. He is that prophet, even Elias,* who, coming after me, is preferred before me, whose shoe's latchet I am not worthy to unloose, *or whose place I am not able to fill; for he shall baptize, not only with water, but with fire, and with the Holy Ghost.*

"29 The next day John seeth Jesus coming unto him, and said; Behold the Lamb of God, who taketh away the sin of the world!

"30 *And John bare record of him unto the people, saying,* This is he of whom I said; After me cometh a man who is preferred before me; for he was before me, and I knew him, *and* that he should be made manifest to Israel; therefore am I come baptizing with water.

"31 And John bare record, saying; *When he was baptized of me,* I saw the Spirit descending from heaven like a dove, and it abode upon him.

"32 And I knew him; for he who sent me to baptize with water, the same said unto me; Upon whom thou shalt see the Spirit descending, and remaining on him, the same is he who baptizeth with the Holy Ghost.

"33 And I saw, and bare record that this is the Son of God.

"34 *These things were done in Bethabara, beyond Jordan, where John was baptizing.*"

I felt impressed that the first verse of the Joseph Smith Translation of John, Chapter One, refers to the Gospel being preached among spirits in pre-mortal life, and that even in pre-mortal life, the gospel was preached to our Heavenly Father's spirit children through his Firstling, Jehovah, the Son.

I believe this is a pattern applied throughout the eternities among all exalted fathers and their respective spirit offspring: The gospel is the same. The ordinances thereof are the same. The plan of redemption is the same. *"Therefore, in the ordinances thereof, the power of godliness is manifest."* (see Doctrine and Covenants 84:20-21)

The spirit firstling of any given exalted father is the atoning agent for all of *that* father's spirit offspring, and as *their* atoning agent, he is also the one through whom the gospel is brought to all of *that* father's spirit offspring, from their pre-mortal estate all the way through their exaltation.

Firstlings are in the bosom of their respective fathers, and are chosen even from when they were all intelligences not yet clothed in spirit bodies. It has ever been so, and will ever be so (see Doctrine and covenants 76:39).

I was also impressed that Doctrine and Covenants 76:39 uses the word *worlds*, plural:

"For all the rest shall be brought forth by the resurrection of the dead, through the triumph and the glory of the Lamb, who was slain, who was in the bosom of the Father before the **worlds** *were made."*

ILLUSTRATION-1

TINKER TOY MODEL OF ETERNAL FAMILY STRUCTURES
CONCEPTUALIZED BY ILYAN KEI LAVANWAY, CIRCA 2016

DIAGRAM KEY: ● EXALTED HUSBAND
                O EXALTED WIFE
                ━ COVENANT BOND OF ETERNAL MARRIAGE
                ||||| SPIRIT CHILDREN

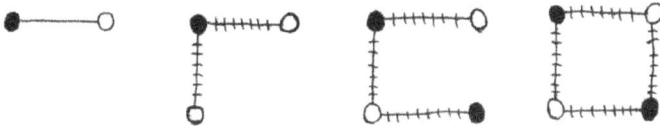

NOTE: FOR SIMPLICITY, CHILDREN ARE NOT SHOWN IN THE EXPANSIONS BELOW:

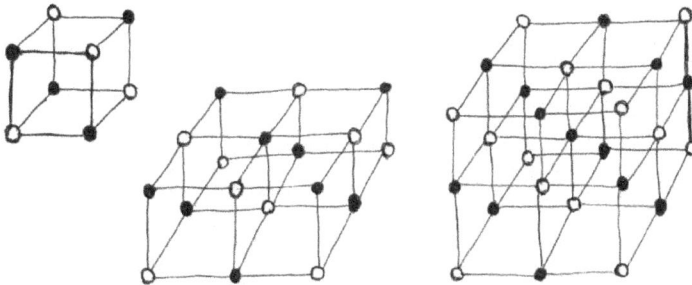

Ilyan Kei Lavanway
11 JANUARY 2019

This page intentionally left blank.

ILLUSTRATION-2

TINKER TOY MODEL OF ETERNAL FAMILY STRUCTURES
CONCEPTUALIZED BY ILYAN KEI LAVANWAY, CIRCA 2016
HYPERCUBE EXPANSION CONCEPTUALIZED 10 JANUARY 2019

Ilyan Kei LaVanway
11 JANUARY 2019

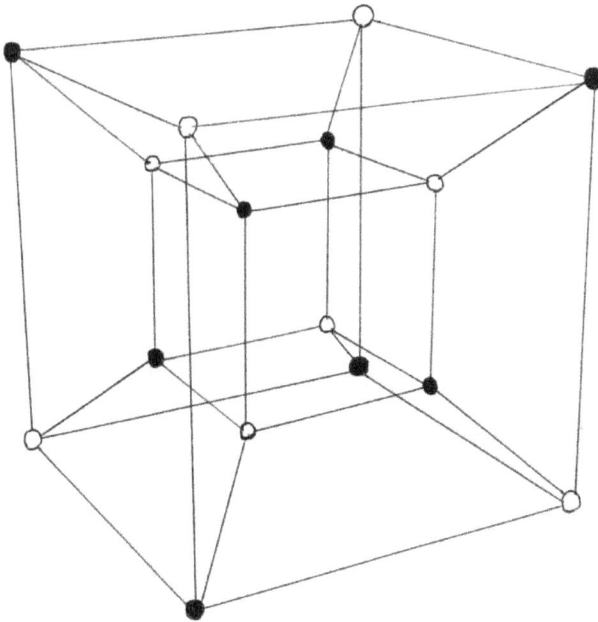

DIAGRAM KEY: ● EXALTED HUSBAND
              ○ EXALTED WIFE
              — COVENANT BOND OF ETERNAL MARRIAGE
              |||| SPIRIT CHILDREN (NOT SHOWN FOR SIMPLICITY)

ILLUSTRATION PAGE 2

This page intentionally left blank.

ILLUSTRATION-3

TINKER TOY MODEL OF ETERNAL FAMILY STRUCTURES
CONCEPTUALIZED BY ILYAN KEI LAVANWAY, CIRCA 2016
SUPERIMPOSED SQUARES CONCEPTUALIZED 11 JANUARY 2019
KEY: ● EXALTED HUSBAND
      ○ EXALTED WIFE
      ▬ COVENANT BOND OF ETERNAL MARRIAGE
      |||| SPIRIT CHILDREN (NOT SHOWN FOR SIMPLICITY)

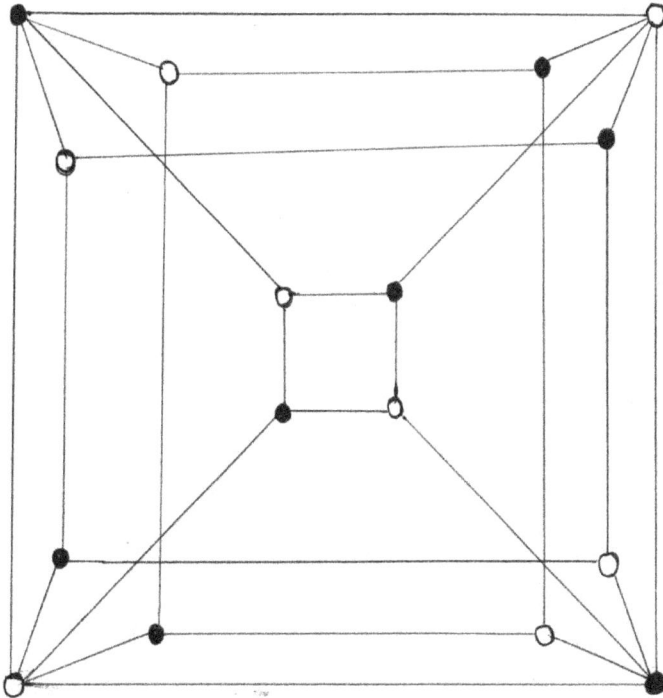

ILLUSTRATION IMPLIES INFINITELY
MANY ETERNAL SPOUSES.

11 JANUARY 2019

ILLUSTRATION PAGE 3

This page intentionally left blank.

ILLUSTRATION-4

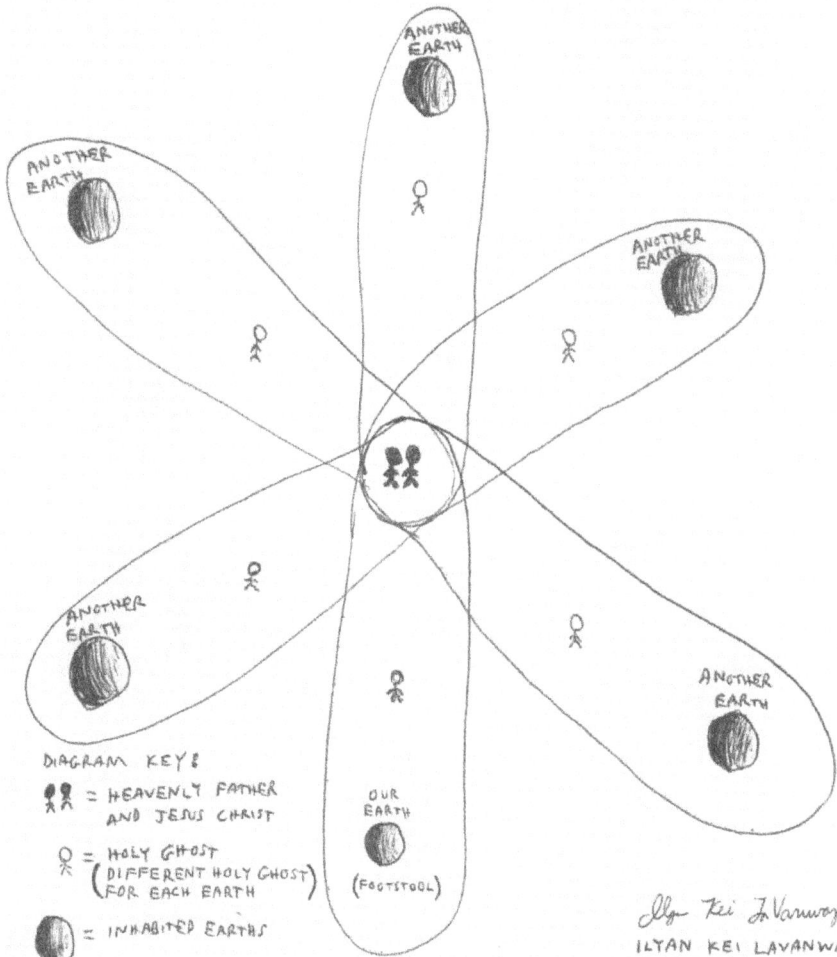

ANOTHER EARTH

ANOTHER EARTH

ANOTHER EARTH

ANOTHER EARTH

ANOTHER EARTH

DIAGRAM KEY:

👫 = HEAVENLY FATHER AND JESUS CHRIST

⚲ = HOLY GHOST (DIFFERENT HOLY GHOST FOR EACH EARTH)

● = INHABITED EARTHS

OUR EARTH

(FOOTSTOOL)

Ilya Kei LaVanway
ILYAN KEI LAVANWAY
29 NOVEMBER 2018

This page intentionally left blank.

ADDITIONAL READING ON RELATED TOPICS

Books by Ilyan Kei Lavanway exploring related subject matter:

Onions of Eternity
ISBN 9781520402222

Intelligent Universe
ISBN 9781494905910

Nature of The Godhead
ISBN 9780463012000

Circumscription Hypothesis
ISBN 9781505429329

Thought Log 2015.08.17.1900
ISBN 9781523422173

The Grandeur of Christmas and The Son of God
ISBN 9781520260082

The Book of Mormon Answers The Fermi Paradox
ISBN 9798586510273

This page intentionally left blank.

WRITTEN WORKS BY ILYAN KEI LAVANWAY

Published:

Eternal Family Structures Among Exalted Couples (2021)

The Book of Mormon Answers The Fermi Paradox (2020)

Cleansing of The Church (2020)

Dreams of the Last Days: Dragons and Clocks (2020)

Dreams of the Last Days: Mobile Tactical Temples (2017)

Dreams of the Last Days: Psychokinetic Flight and Pyrokinesis (2016)

Dreams of the Last Days: Marked and Messaged (2015)

Dreams of the last Days: Machines and Machinations (2015)

Dreams of the Last Days: Where are all the Stars? (2015)

Vanishing Room (2019)

An Aviator At Heart (2014, 2019)

Nature of the Godhead (2019)

Guidebook for Your Journey Home (2017)

Onions of Eternity (2017)

The Grandeur of Christmas and The Son of God (2016)

Paradise and Spirit Prison (2016)

What Happens at the Second Coming of Jesus Christ (2016)

Thought Log 2015.08.17.1900 (2016)

The Lowliest of Callings (2016)

Families are Meant to Last Forever (2016)

Dream Log 2015.09.18.0900 (2015)

Thought Log 2015.08.09.2100 (2015)

Baptism by Immersion in Water and in the Spirit of God (2015)

Likening My Life to the Apostle Dieter Friedrich Uchtdorf (2015)

If Christ had not Suffered (2015)

Honoring His Namesake (2015)

FEMA Camp Parent Trap (2015)

Marriage (2015)

Relying on the Lord in the Last Days (2015)

Circumscription Hypothesis (2015)

Intelligent Universe (2014)

Sevenfold (2013)

The Modern Day Gadianton Golden Boy (2012)

Post Omerican Easter (2012)

Duck Boy on the Platypus Farm (2012)

Platypus Boy on the Duck Farm (2012)

Into the Picture (2012)

Earth Sink (2010)

Chicken Poop From the Hole (2005)

Unpublished (Note: this list is not complete):

Personal Impressions Scripture Study Log: 2019 Edition (2020)

100-Word Flash Fiction Collection (2018)

You Cannot Wield Your Way with a Sword of Sand (2018)

Fast Offerings: The Lord's Way of Blessing Both Giver and Receiver (2017)

Knit Together as One (2017)

Object-Generated Wormholes as Wake Effect Causing Superluminal Transit (2017)

Cinderella Cruella (2017)

Keeping the Sabbath Day Holy: Sacrament Meeting (2017)

Facebook Conversation about Adam and Eve (2016)

Dream Log 2016.12.24.0600 (2016)

The Parable of the Ten Virgins for Our Day (2016)

A Great American Dichotomy (2016)

States of the Flesh (2016)

Home Teaching: The Meat of the Gospel (2016)

Missionary Successes Visible and Invisible (2016)

Obey the Commandments of God (2016)

A Lesson from Job for Our Day (2016)

Why the Word of Wisdom Warns us to Avoid Coffee and Tea (2016)

The Atonement Affords Access to Parallel Realities (2016)

Is a New Age Deception Poisoning Some of the Elect? (2016)

Thoughts on the Benefits of Asking for a Priesthood Blessing (2016)

Soul Reacher (2012)

This page intentionally left blank.

AUTHOR CONTACT

Email:
ilyanlavanway@gmail.com

Amazon Author Page:
https://www.amazon.com/author/ilyan
https://www.amazon.com/Ilyan-Kei-Lavanway/e/B004YL1HG2

Smashwords Author Page:
https://www.smashwords.com/profile/view/ilyan

Goodreads Author Page:
https://www.goodreads.com/author/show/4751470.Ilyan_Kei_Lavanway

LinkedIn:
https://www.linkedin.com/in/ilyanlavanway/

Twitter:
@ilyanlavanway
https://twitter.com/ilyanlavanway
@dare2unveil
https://twitter.com/dare2unveil

Website:
https://www.cajunostomy.com

This page intentionally left blank.

www.ingramcontent.com/pod-product-compliance
Lightning Source LLC
Chambersburg PA
CBHW031334040426

42443CB00005B/345